Y0-BVQ-648

CITY AND SUBURB

CITY AND SUBURB

EXPLORING AN ECOSYSTEM

BY LAURENCE PRINGLE

MACMILLAN PUBLISHING CO., INC.
New York
COLLIER MACMILLAN PUBLISHERS
London

Macmillan Publishing Co., Inc.,
866 Third Avenue, New York, N.Y. 10022
Collier Macmillan Canada, Ltd.
Printed in the United States of America

1   2   3   4   5   6   7   8   9   10

Library of Congress Cataloging in Publication Data
Pringle, Laurence P   City and suburb.
        Bibliography: p.   Includes index.
1. Urban ecology (Biology)—Juvenile literature.
    [1. Urban ecology (Biology)   2. Ecology.
3. Nature study]   I. Title.   QH541.5.C6P74
                        574.5′09173′2   75–16161
                            ISBN 0–02–775350–6

For the late Raymond E. Francis,
who helped me on my way

ABOUT THIS BOOK

An ecosystem is a place in nature with all of its living and nonliving parts. Ecosystems are all around us. Some are big, some are little. The planet earth is one ecosystem, a rotting log is another. Ponds, forests, and estuaries are ecosystems too. A city with its suburbs is also an ecosystem, and one we know little about.

In order to understand nature, ecologists usually study ponds, forests, and other ecosystems that have not been disturbed very much by humans. Perhaps it is time to learn more about the ecosystems where most people work and live.

A city-suburb is a complex place. The shape of the land and even the climate have been changed by people. Plants and animals from other countries have replaced some of those that lived in the area before. But there are also many clues to the kinds of ecosystems that existed before the city-suburb was built.

City-suburb ecosystems are places of bricks and brooks, cats and cattails, rats and raccoons. Go see for yourself. A city-suburb is a fascinating world to explore.

Sometimes a city seems to be entirely man-made—a world of crowded streets, blaring horns, and neon signs. The land is covered with concrete, macadam, stone, brick, wood, steel, and glass. Hills have been leveled and valleys filled in. Rivers have been polluted and straightened, their banks lined with concrete.

Look again. Look in parks, in vacant lots, in sidewalk cracks, in patches of earth along roadsides. There you can find trees, wildflowers, insects, birds, snakes, and mammals.

Look closely at the stems of plants in a vacant lot. You may see a ladybug eating aphids.

City-suburb ecosystems are a strange mixture of living and nonliving things. One way to understand this mixture is to trace the changes that occur as a city grows. Most cities in North America began at a crossroads or harbor, places where trade and travel were convenient. At first, people got most of their food and fuel from nearby farms and forests. As land was cleared and buildings put up, the habitat (living place) of many plants and animals was changed or destroyed. But wolves, bears, and other wildlife still lived nearby, in the surrounding wilderness.

As the population grew, cities got bigger and changed in other ways. Trains and ships brought food and fuels from faraway places. Low, wooden buildings were replaced by taller ones of concrete and steel. Cities became less and less like the ecosystems that existed before. But open land and wild places could still be found just beyond the city line.

The automobile changed all that. Once cars became common, streets were paved, parking lots were built, and highways reached out into the surrounding countryside. People discovered that they could live in the country and commute to their jobs in the city. As more and more people did this, however, the "country" became more and more like the city they had left. Gradually, industries moved to the suburbs, and many people found jobs in the suburbs themselves. Today, the numbers of people living in most cities have stopped increasing, while suburban populations are growing rapidly.

The top aerial photo shows part of Long Island, New York, in 1947. It was mostly farmland then. The bottom photo shows the same scene in 1974—covered with houses and factories.

As suburbs spread farther and farther from the centers of cities, they began to bump up against the sprawling suburbs of other cities. The result is a new kind of human settlement—the metropolitan area. A modern metropolis can be a hundred times larger in area than the biggest cities that existed before the invention of the automobile.

The differences between city and suburb are becoming blurred as the suburbs become more densely settled. Some suburbs have high-rise buildings and traffic jams. In fact, suburbs near big cities often have less open space and more "city problems" than smaller cities that are not so densely settled.

MOTEL
EVRON
DEALER
RKCHESTER
MOTEL
For Less
ULTI-COUPLE
UNITS
KITCHENETTES
POOL
URN HERE
OL TV APTS
FAMILY UN TS SITER
KITCHENETTES
PARK BOA S TRAIL
VACANCY
LIQUORS
TEXA O
B&E
TO PARTS
UTEL
FURNITURE
AUTO
ARTS

In some ways, cities are unlike forests, ponds, and other ecosystems. In most ecosystems, the food used by animals comes mostly from the ecosystem itself. In a city-suburb, however, the common large mammals—humans—get nearly all of their food from outside the area where they live. The food often grows hundreds or thousands of miles away.

Also, in a forest or pond, there is no such thing as waste. Every bit of dead plant or animal material is used by some living thing. The minerals and other nutrients from once-living things are recycled again and again, and usually stay within the ecosystem. In a city-suburb, people think of garbage as a nuisance. Wastes are burned, buried, or dumped into lakes or rivers. In small amounts they enrich the land and waters. Often, however, there is so much garbage that it causes pollution.

Some of the food we eat comes from ecosystems in other states, or even other countries.

Like all ecosystems, a city-suburb affects its surroundings and is affected by them. But compared with other ecosystems, the effects of a city-suburb are far-reaching. Think of the food, fuels, clothing, chairs, bicycles, and all of the other objects of everyday life. Ecosystems on the other side of the earth may be farmed or mined to produce them.

You can see many of the ways in which a city affects its surroundings as highways are built, forests cut down, and ponds filled in or polluted. But a city has other, less obvious effects. It affects the climate for miles around, and even makes its own climate.

In Maryland, a suburb replaces a forest. It is part of the Washington, D.C., metropolitan area.

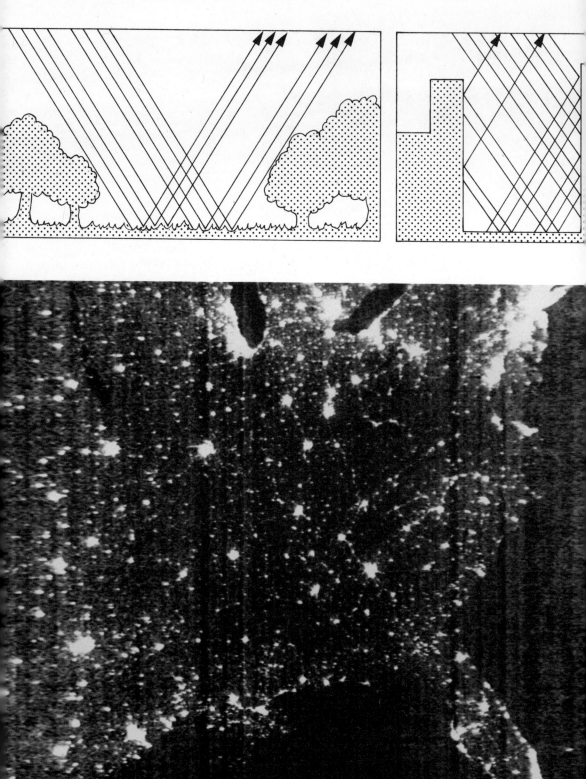

In open countryside, most of the sun's rays are reflected from plants or the ground back into the atmosphere. In a city, the rays are often reflected from a building, to the pavement, up to another building, and so on. The buildings, streets, and parking lots absorb heat from the sun. Some of this heat warms the surrounding air. At night the bricks, concrete, and other hard materials lose their heat slowly, so the city remains warmer than the surrounding countryside.

People make a city even more of a "heat island" by using great amounts of energy in industries, automobiles, and appliances. Waste heat from the use of energy adds to heat from the sun. Because of this effect, a city-suburb is warmer on weekdays than on Sundays, when fewer people are working and using fuels.

In the country (top left), most of the sun's rays are reflected back into the atmosphere. In a city (top right), the rays are reflected from one surface to another, raising the temperature of the surrounding area. The photo below, taken from a weather satellite at night, shows the lights of metropolitan areas in the eastern United States.

Scientists are studying city heat islands. They observed the climate when the new town of Columbia, Maryland, was built. Between 1967 and 1974, the population of the area grew from 200 to 25,000. A heat island was created. Temperatures in Columbia are sometimes 14° F higher than the surrounding countryside.

Some of the known effects of heat islands are startling. For example, the growing season in Washington, D.C., is a month longer than that of nearby rural areas. When a country snowstorm reaches a city, it often changes to sleet or rain. And areas that are downwind from a heat island have more precipitation than other areas around a city. The effects of a heat island are worst during several days of hot summer weather. The city air does not cool off much during the night, and some people become ill and even die because of the heat.

Even a "cooling" rain shower doesn't help a city much. In the country, many raindrops stay on plants and on the ground. As this water evaporates, it cools both the land and the air. Most city rainwater is quickly carried off by sewers, so there's little left to evaporate.

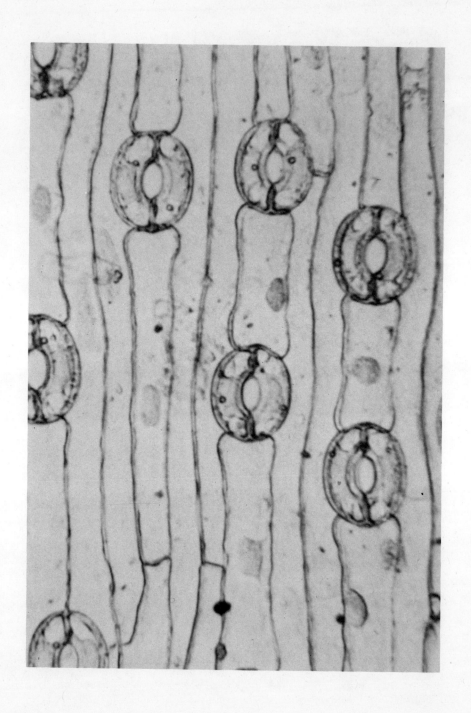

City air has more dust particles and harmful chemicals than country air. Sunlight reflects off the particles, so less sunlight reaches the city-suburb than reaches open country. The amount of sunlight reaching Washington, D.C., has dropped 16 percent in the last fifty years. Because of the particles in the air, cities have more cloudy days and more fog than the countryside around them.

Air pollution reaches beyond a city's borders, damaging crops and killing trees. Most trees cannot survive the polluted air. The tiny openings in the leaves of many kinds of trees become clogged with dirt, and they cannot take in the air they need. This is especially bad for evergreens. Their needles (leaves) remain alive and exposed to the harmful effects of pollution for several years. Deciduous trees, which replace their leaves each year, have a better chance for survival.

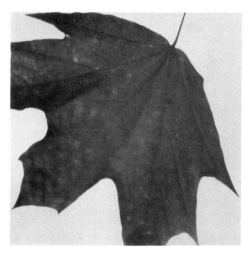

The doughnut-shaped holes (left) are stomata—tiny openings through which gases pass in and out of leaves. There are thousands of stomata on the underside of a single maple leaf (right).

Polluted air also affects city animals, although very little is known about this. The bodies of city pigeons contain two to five times as much lead (from gasoline) as rural pigeons. City dogs have more lung diseases than country dogs. When pollution is at its worst, the health of dogs and pet birds is definitely affected, and some die.

Some city trees die for lack of water. Since much of the surface of the land in a city-suburb is made watertight by pavement and buildings, rainwater has little chance to soak into the ground.

Without knowing it, people have a great effect on living things in the city. Usually we are concerned only with our pets, with our gardens and lawns (if we have them), and with such pests as cockroaches. We are not aware of the hundreds of other kinds of living things that surround us, or of how we affect their lives and how they affect ours.

Rain in the city has little chance to soak into the ground.

No matter how big a city is, you can find wild animals and plants within it. Harmless garter snakes, milkweed plants with downy seeds, and scurrying sowbugs live in many city-suburbs.

As a metropolitan area grows and spreads, the numbers and kinds of wild animals and plants decrease as their habitats disappear. You can see this process happening in suburbs as they become more and more like cities. In 1965, deer were sometimes seen in wooded parts of Tenafly, New Jersey, just a few miles from Manhattan, the heart of the New York City metropolitan area. Then a golf course was built in a neighboring community. Many acres of forest were cut down. The deer lost a key part of their habitat and no longer live in that part of New Jersey.

A deer needs a large area of wild land in order to survive. Other wild mammals are better able to adapt to drastic changes in their habitat. Raccoons, skunks, and opossums live within the borders of most North American cities and are common in surrounding suburbs. Coyotes, found in several western cities, are especially abundant in Los Angeles, California.

In 1968, a raccoon was found in the ventilation system of an office building in downtown Cincinnati, Ohio. This aroused the interest of two biologists, who then studied the raccoons that lived in a 320-acre area of the city. They found one raccoon for about every nine acres of land: the city raccoons were as abundant as rural raccoons.

The Cincinnati raccoons had dens in a wooded section of the city, but they also made dens in storm sewers, attics, and garages. One female raised her young on a sofa on the unused third floor of a house. The raccoons often traveled from place to place through the city's storm sewer system. They found some of their food there, but mostly ate garbage taken from trash cans, or scraps left deliberately by people. In most other ways, city-suburb raccoons are like raccoons that live in swamps and other wild, undisturbed ecosystems.

Gulls thrive near cities because garbage is plentiful.
Magpies (right) live on the outskirts of many western cities.

Other kinds of animals, and plants, have adapted well to an urban environment. Crows live in suburbs and within some cities. They can often be seen searching for food along the edges of highways. Squirrels are plentiful in parks and forested cemeteries. Chimney swifts nest and roost in chimneys, rather than in hollow trees as they do in wilderness areas.

Many city-suburb animals are omnivores: they eat both plants and other animals. Many are scavengers: they eat dead things. And people give them plenty to eat. Large flocks of herring gulls live near some metropolitan areas. They feast on the garbage that people throw away. So do raccoons, rats, mice, pigeons, and cockroaches.

Cockroaches first came to North America as stowaways on sailing ships. They are just one kind of organism that people have introduced—sometimes on purpose, sometimes not—to the city-suburb ecosystem. Rats and house mice have followed humans and shared their living places for centuries. During the 1800s, starlings and house sparrows were brought to eastern North America. They have since spread to almost all cities and suburbs, where they compete for food with pigeons, another bird brought from Europe. Late in the 1960s, the monk parakeet came accidentally to the United States. It eats fruit and corn, and may become a pest in suburban gardens.

City streets are often a tough environment for trees, but people have found a few species that do well despite the polluted air. Among the most common is the London plane tree. It is closely related to the sycamore, a native tree, but is better able to survive in cities. Living conditions for trees are better in city parks and in suburbs, so most trees there are native to North America.

Cockroaches need food, warmth, moisture, and places to hide. Without meaning to, we often give them ideal habitats in our homes.

About 75 different kinds of eucalyptus trees from Australia now grow in cities in southern California. They have such names as blue gum, red gum, and red ironbark. The leaves curl up on hot days, losing little moisture to the air; the big taproot grows deep into the soil. In ways like these, eucalyptus trees do well where water is scarce.

In eastern cities, the ailanthus, a native of China, is found in alleys, vacant lots, and just about anywhere it can find a little soil, water, and sunlight. Ailanthus leaves are the favorite food of the caterpillars that later develop into cynthia moths. These big Asian moths live wherever the ailanthus grows.

The cynthia moth has a wingspread of five inches.

Wild flowers grow along roadsides and in other open spaces.

Grasses and weeds grow wherever a little soil is exposed, though their roots may have to grope through a crack in concrete in order to reach the earth. Tangled wild gardens cover vacant lots. These weeds are a mixture of native species and those brought from other countries or other parts of our continent. Asters, milkweed, and goldenrods grew in open spaces before people built cities in North America. Ragweed, a native of the western plains, now thrives in eastern cities.

But most city-suburb weeds were brought from Europe, either on purpose or by accident. Crab grass, English plan-

Weeds thrive where many other plants would die. U. S. 1878806

tain, and Russian thistle now grow in New York City, Denver, Los Angeles, and many other cities. All of these plants —native or alien—have one thing in common: they are able to grow and reproduce under difficult conditions. A city is no place for tender plants.

Many city-suburb weeds have beautiful flowers. Some have edible leaves, seeds, or roots. Salads, soups, beverages, and vegetable dishes can be made from the wild gardens of alleys, vacant lots, and roadsides. But the plant parts should always be washed first, to remove the coating of soot and oil that settles out of the air.

The numbers of plants and animals change with time. Recently, the populations of dogs and cats have been increasing. These mammals are more than just pets; they affect other living things in the city-suburb ecosystem. In New York City alone, as much as 20,000 tons of dog droppings are left on sidewalks and streets each year. These wastes are breeding places for houseflies, which carry diseases that affect people. Rain washes the droppings through storm sewers and into rivers and lakes, further polluting the water.

Most dogs and cats are well cared for, but many thousands are abandoned and left to fend for themselves. Some strays are rounded up, some are killed by cars, and some survive as wild animals. (A tame animal that turns wild is called feral.)

Feral cats near the Fulton Fish Market in New York City

A biologist named Alan Beck spent several years observing the feral dogs of Baltimore, Maryland. In many ways the dogs behaved like foxes or other wild animals. They usually stayed within a certain territory, seeking food from garbage cans or getting handouts from people. In summer they might find water under a dripping air conditioner.

Dr. Beck spent a lot of time watching one dog, which he named Shag. He followed Shag and other dogs, observing their lives.

Dr. Beck soon learned that feral dogs are usually most active early in the morning and in the evening. After many weeks of observing Shag and other dogs, he learned a lot about their regular routes, their favorite resting and denning places, and the dangers in their lives. He also became very fond of Shag and was upset when Shag disappeared late one fall. There was no sign of the dog for six weeks. Then one day Shag reappeared—at the end of a leash. A man had adopted Shag, and a feral dog was tame once more.

A feral dog in Denver, ready to flee
from the photographer

Cats become feral too, and probably survive better than dogs. Whether feral or tame, both cats and dogs go hunting when they have a chance. Dogs chase squirrels and rabbits. In the outer suburbs they sometimes form packs and go after bigger prey, such as deer. House cats stalk ground squirrels, songbirds, chipmunks, and mice. Dogs and cats have been hunters since ancient times. In city-suburb eco-systems, cats and dogs take the place, in part, of the owls,

weasels, foxes, and bobcats that were common predators in the past.

Like all ecosystems, a city-suburb changes with time. Animals and plants come and go, their numbers rise or fall as changes affect their habitat. Old buildings are replaced with modern ones, usually without window ledges on which pigeons can build their nests. This may eventually reduce the numbers of pigeons.

As suburbs spread outward from cities, there is a drop in the numbers of birds and other animals that live in forests, farmland, and meadows. But there is an increase in the numbers of animals (such as robins and mockingbirds) that live among lawns and shrubs. As a result of air pollution controls and more careful use of insect poisons, increasing numbers of butterflies and insect-eating birds are seen in some cities. The patterns of life keep changing.

As you walk along a city street, it may be hard to imagine that deer and wolves once lived there. All you may see is an ant on the sidewalk, but all cities have parks, vacant lots, cemeteries, backyards, and other relatively wild places.

Some city parks are so small or so overused that they support only a few kinds of plants and animals. Others are big enough or better protected, so that little pockets of wildness remain. More than 260 species of birds have been seen in New York City's Central Park. It is a place where you can also see dragonflies and catch tadpoles.

When a biologist studied the gray squirrels of Central Park, he discovered that their numbers were highest near the border and entrances, where people fed them. The squirrels also suffered from eye diseases and fur loss because they ate mostly one kind of food, peanuts.

Some city parks have only a few trees, birds, or squirrels (left). Others are rich with wildlife, including frogs, minnows, and water insects.

Cemeteries are especially good places to find wild animals. They are quiet, safe places, less used by people than most parks. Many older cemeteries have full-grown trees in which crows, owls, squirrels, and raccoons make their nests or dens.

Fifty cemeteries take up 35 percent of the land in the city of Boston and its suburbs. When biologists studied the wild animals in these cemeteries, they saw 95 different species of birds and found the nests of 35 species. They also counted 20 different kinds of mammals, as well as snakes, turtles, frogs, and many insect species. The biologists were surprised at the numbers and variety of animals they found, even in densely settled parts of the city. One wrote, "Imagine standing in a 3-acre cemetery in south-central Boston, surrounded by 5- to 12-story buildings, seeing a sparrow hawk deliver a meal of freshly killed rodent to its young."

The city-suburb has more life than most people realize. It may have fewer *kinds* of plants and animals than a pond or forest. In that way it is a simple ecosystem. But in another way, it is the most complex of all ecosystems—a mixture of lifeless, man-made structures, plants and animals brought from afar, and native survivors from past ecosystems. It is a new kind of ecosystem—one that we know little about. But it is close at hand, waiting to be discovered.

The ailanthus, from China, grows quickly in almost any kind of soil. It survives where no native tree could live.

GLOSSARY

CLIMATE—the average weather conditions of an area, including temperature, windiness, amount of rain and other precipitation, amount of water vapor in the air, and hours of sunlight.

DECIDUOUS—a plant that periodically loses all of its leaves, usually in the autumn. A few "evergreens," such as larch and cypress, are also deciduous.

ECOLOGY—the study of relationships between living things and their environment.

ECOSYSTEM—a place in nature with all of its living and nonliving parts, including soils and climate. The earth is one huge ecosystem. Other ecosystems include forests, deserts, ponds, puddles, and rotting logs.

ENVIRONMENT—all of the surroundings of an organism, including other living things, soils, water, and climate.

ESTUARY—a place where salt water and fresh water mix, usually where ocean tides enter a river. Estuaries are usually called bays, sounds, harbors, or lagoons.

EVAPORATION—the process of a liquid changing to a gas (vapor).

FERAL ANIMAL—a tame animal, such as a dog or cat, that escapes or is abandoned and lives the life of a wild animal.

HABITAT—the living place or immediate surroundings of an organism. If an animal's habitat is changed or destroyed, the animal usually dies (unless it can adapt to the changes).

HEAT ISLAND—a mass of warm air over a city or metropolitan area. The heat is partly wasted energy from machines and partly solar energy that is absorbed by buildings, streets, and other structures.

METROPOLITAN AREA—a city and its surrounding suburbs. A major metropolitan area may include several cities and dozens of suburban towns. The New York City metropolitan area covers 6,900 square miles in three states and has over 16 million residents.

NUTRIENT—a substance, such as calcium, that is needed for the normal growth and development of an organism.

OMNIVORE—an animal that eats both plants and other animals.

POLLUTION—people-produced wastes, such as heat, noise, sewage, and poisons, that lower the quality of the environment.

PREDATOR—an animal that kills other animals for food.

SCAVENGER—an animal that feeds on the remains of dead plants or animals.

TERRITORY—an area lived in by an animal, pair of animals, or group of animals, and defended by them against intruders. Many kinds of birds and mammals, including dogs and cats, maintain territories.

FURTHER READING

Books marked with an asterisk (*) are fairly simple; the others are more difficult.

*ANONYMOUS. "Life in a City Lot." *Ranger Rick's Nature Magazine,* October 1972, pp. 18–21.

*BECK, ALAN M. "The Life and Times of Shag, a Feral Dog in Baltimore." *Natural History,* October 1971, pp. 58–65.

*CAULEY, DARRELL L. AND SCHINNER, JAMES R. "The Cincinnati Raccoons." *Natural History,* November 1973, pp. 58–60.

*COHEN, DANIEL. *Animals of the City.* New York: McGraw-Hill, 1969.

*COLE, JOANNA. *Cockroaches.* New York: Morrow, 1971.

*DOWDEN, ANNE OPHELIA. *Wild Green Things in the City: A Book of Weeds.* New York: Thomas Y. Crowell, 1972.

GILL, DON AND BONNETT, PENELOPE. *Nature in the Urban Landscape: A Study of City Ecosystems.* Baltimore: York Press, 1973.

KINKEAD, EUGENE. *A Concrete Look at Nature.* New York: Quadrangle Books, 1974.

*MARTIN, ALEXANDER C. *Weeds* (A Golden Nature Guide). New York: Golden Press, 1973.

PETERSON, JAMES T. *"Energy and the Weather."* Environment, October 1973, pp. 4–9.

*PRINGLE, LAURENCE. *Ecology: Science of Survival.* New York: Macmillan, 1971.

*PRINGLE, LAURENCE. *Into the Woods: Exploring the Forest Ecosystem.* New York: Macmillan, 1973.

RUBLOWSKY, JOHN. *Nature in the City.* New York: Basic Books, 1967.

SIMON, SEYMOUR. *Science in a Vacant Lot.* New York: Viking Press, 1970.

*THOMAS, JACK W. AND DIXON, RONALD A. "Cemetery Ecology." *Natural History*, March 1973, pp. 61–67.

INDEX

An asterisk (*) indicates a photograph or drawing

PICTURE CREDITS

ALSO BY LAURENCE PRINGLE